Ueno Mornings

John Gribble

Ueno Mornings
© 2015 John Gribble
All rights reserved.

Wordrunner Press
ISBN: 978-1-941066-05-8

Cover image: Kan'ei Temple,
detail from *Edo oezu*,
published by Nishimuraya Yohachi, 1863
Courtesy of David Rumsey Map Collection
www.davidrumsey.com

For permission or to comment
contact gribblej@gol.com

Book design:
Jo-Anne Rosen
www.wordrunner.com

My thanks go first and foremost to my wife Miwako for her patient, good-humored help and support. The members of the Tokyo Writers Workshop and the "G7" poets group have helped immeasurably with this and all my writing over the years. I am blessed on all sides.

This collection is dedicated to my friends, colleagues, and students, past and present, at Tokyo Geijutsu Daigaku.

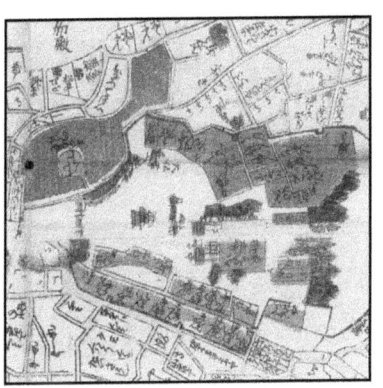

Ueno Mornings

brown branch
red leaves
black crow

cold morning—
even the homeless move
with purpose

a baby stroller
full of rags
homeless woman

museum poster—
a wooden emperor's
wooden stare

a few pigeons
a few umbrellas
mostly rain

morning patrol—
dark blue officers,
light blue tents

museum poster—
homely women Rembrandt knew
on display inside

behind the building
a juggler practices
in private

accustomed to it
the pigeons hold their ground
when the kid charges

double bass
on a luggage cart—
squeaky wheel

the old gate open
the garden finally visible
to visiting dignitaries

an art student
in a bowling shirt & cowboy hat—
tradition

through spiderweb limbs
a tall green bronze warrior—
groundsmen trim the shrubs

thru the trees
a wind shakes
the rain loose

small glade
cool after a rainstorm
the smell of urine

among
the blue tarp tents
one tan Coleman

grey pigeons
in grey water
on black asphalt

a fistfight—
last night's unfinished business
continues this morning

Rodin's "Burghers"
suspended from a crane,
grey quilts over all their heads

canteen —
he drinks the water for later
now

a cat stalking
a pigeon, interrupted
by a petting

apron & pants—
a housewife
but homeless

on new benches
with armrests the homeless
doze upright

red caps, yellow caps,
little troopers in long lines—
off to see Panda!

young mothers,
babies held close, watch
junior high kids

her hair
swings one way, violin case
the other

hands smooth bushy hair,
then straighten navy school suits
take the picture — now!

museum gate
where a proud beagle
gets brushed

brooms leaned against
a tree, the ground freshly swept
around it

deepening lines
above a small diamond
necklace

homeless cats
on leashes
in trees

an old woman
hurries past—
fresh soap smell

a workman
first lectures, then feeds
the pigeons

at the urinal
next to me a man wears
a horsehead mask

large poster—
a buxom art nouveau
dragonfly

a grinning man holds his eye
against a broken camera—
police await an ambulance

a solo saxophone
in need of relacquering
and lots of practice

rebellion —
after office-bound decades,
a grey ponytail

artwork Buddha
with a broken halo—
museum poster

4 old women
with 1 old man
who smiles

two cameras,
a special vest, stalking
blossoms

toddler
unhinged
in her rage

an old man
straddles his bike, studies
an elephant's portrait

big crowds and big shows:
see the history of
the vacuum tube

a flapping shadow,
my trenchcoat and unstrapped bag—
a large foolish bird

the dogs acquainted,
the owner of one scoops the poop
of the other

Postscript

Ueno Park, the setting of these poem, is officially known as *Ueno Onshi Kôen*, "Ueno Imperial Gift Park." A three-hundred-acre public space in central Tokyo, it is visited by around ten million people a year. The land was once the grounds of Kan'ei Temple. Founded in 1625, the temple prospered under the Tokugawa shogunate, Japan's rulers from 1600 to 1868. But in the 1868-69 Boshin War, the Tokugawa forces were defeated by those supporting the Imperial family. During the Battle of Ueno (July 4, 1868), most the Kan'ei Temple buildings were destroyed.

The property became a possession of the Meiji Emperor. There were various ideas for the use of the land, including a medical school and hospital. But one Anthonius Franciscus Bauduin (1820-1885), a Dutch medical doctor then in Japan, urged the area be turned into a Western-style park. In 1873 Ueno Park was established. It was managed by various Imperial and national agencies until 1924. At that time, in honor of the marriage of then-Crown Prince Hirohito, Ueno Park was presented to the city of Tokyo by the Taishô Emperor.

In the park are a few vestiges of the old temple complex, several major national and municipal museums, two concert halls, Japan's first zoo, various bodies of water, a baseball field named for the poet Shiki Masaoka, and almost nine thousand *sakura*, blooming cherry trees. There is also a sizeable settlement of homeless squatters which dates back to World War II. Adjacent to the park are the main campuses of two major universities, Tokyo University (commonly known as *Todai*) and Tokyo University of the Arts (*Geidai*).

While walking through Ueno Park to Geidai to teach I wrote at least one poem, often more, every Tuesday morning for a couple years. When I found I was repeating myself and stopped, I'd written well over three hundred poems. While nearly all look like three-line English haiku, for the most part I had purposefully avoided counting syllables, using *kigo* (season words) or following other traditional Japanese conventions. I simply looked, felt, tasted, heard, smelled, and wrote. The results were unmeasured, unrhymed imagistic tercets. I jokingly called the material a non-haiku non-sequence.

Reading and rereading the poems, I became convinced they suggested the shape of the writer's mind. I believed that would be a useful organizing principle. There were also *leitmotifs*, reappearing themes, images, and phrases.

I printed out a copy of the manuscript, cut it into one-poem strips, choose poems, then arranged and rearranged them, sliding them around on the dining room table. When I thought I had a section in pretty good order, I taped the poems together.

But none of the versions hung together very well. People I showed the work to were mostly unimpressed. Dissatisfied, I'd start all over, each time with a new, more complicated scheme. Finally I got tired of making myself crazy and put the whole mess away.

Two things brought me back to the project. First was working with poet-translator Masaya Saito on translations of Hashi Kanseki's haiku. We looked at hundreds of Hashi's poems and I came to appreciate his mind, his sensibilities. The mind was revealed, not by some overarching structure or intent, but by the cumulative effect of the poems. Reflecting back on my abandoned project, I began to see how egotistical my approach had been. The focus had been on the poet (read: *me*), not the poems or their subjects.

The new approach was to pick poems which stood up on their own three little legs, gather together some which seemed to play well with others, and attempt to find a kind of "inevitability"(Saito-san's helpful word) in the ordering. It is hoped the poet's mind (read: *ego*) is no longer the point of the work.

The second prompt was more personal and, in a tiny way, historical. My regular walks through Ueno Park will end with my retirement this academic year. In addition, the section of the park the poems depict has changed in the fifteen years since the poems were written. After massive renovation, the old fountain and reflecting pool across from the National Museum are gone. The replacement is smaller and, I think, more attractive. The homeless are still a presence, but their settlement is somewhere else. Where blue tarp tents stood, the work of young sculptors is on display. For better or worse, a restaurant and a Starbucks are now part of the scenery. So the collection documents a place and time now past or passing.

John Gribble
Nishi Tokyo, Tokyo
Autumn, 2014

John Gribble is a Southern Californian who has resided in Tokyo since 1993. His work appears in journals and collections in the US, UK, Australia, Canada, and Japan. A Pushcart nominee, he holds an MFA from Warren Wilson College and is an organizer of both the annual Japan Writers Conference and the Tokyo Writers Workshop. Visit his website at johngribble.com.

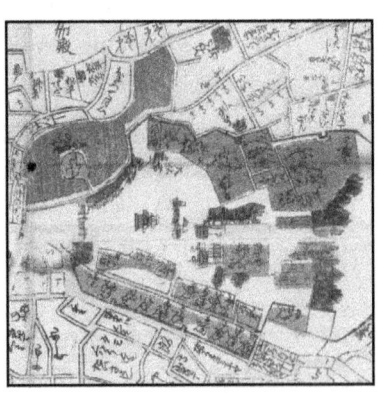

www.ingramcontent.com/pod-product-compliance
Lightning Source LLC
Chambersburg PA
CBHW022345040426
42449CB00006B/720